SOCIAL MEDIA MASTERY GUIDE

Social Media Mastery Guide

YOUR PATH TO DIGITAL TRIUMPH

Ebony A. Singletary

Ebony Azuri Consulting LLC

Contents

Dedication   vi

1 Introduction   1

2 Understanding Your Audience   6

3 Choosing the Right Platforms   11

4 Crafting A Winning Strategy   16

5 Creating Compelling Content   21

6 Building an Engaged Community   26

7 Mastering Hashtags and Trends   31

8 Influencer Collaboration   34

9 Paid Social Advertising   37

10 Analyzing and Optimizing   42

11 Staying Ahead of Trends   47

12 Case Studies and Success Stories   53

13 Crafting Your Comprehensive Social Media Plan   58

14 Resources and Tools   63

About The Author   66

To my dearest husband,

You are the unwavering anchor in the tempest of life, the silent supporter in the crescendo of dreams. This book is dedicated to you, my pillar of strength, the one who not only gives me the space to shine but illuminates the path with your boundless love and encouragement.

In every endeavor and dream I wish to reach, you stand beside me, a steadfast ally, the wind beneath my wings propelling me to new heights. Your support is the melody that harmonizes with my aspirations, creating a symphony of shared dreams and achievements.

You are the embodiment of God's love in my life, a reflection of grace, kindness, and unwavering devotion. With each page of this book, know that your love is woven into the fabric of every word, every insight, and every lesson shared.

I love you to the moon and back, beyond the stars and into the infinite expanse of our shared journey. Thank you for being the compass that guides me and the anchor that grounds me. This book is as much yours as it is mine, a testament to the beautiful journey we continue to embark upon together.

With all my love,

Ebony

1

Introduction

Defining Your Target Audience

Successful social media marketing begins with understanding your target audience. Defining your target audience is the cornerstone of a successful social media marketing strategy. It identifies the people most likely to resonate with your brand, products, or services. This step is about broad demographics and understanding your potential customers' deeper characteristics, behaviors, interests, and pain points. By delving into the specifics of your target audience, you gain insights that allow you to tailor your content, messaging, and engagement strategies precisely. This targeted approach ensures that your efforts resonate more profoundly, making your brand stand out in a sea of content. Whether creating compelling visuals, writing persuasive copy, or interacting with followers, clearly understanding your target audience allows you to connect personally, fostering trust and loyalty.

The benefits of defining your target audience extend beyond resonating with your customers – it also maximizes your return on investment. Resources are valuable, and targeting the right audience ensures you direct your efforts where they matter most. With a well-defined audience, you can allocate your budget and resources effectively, reaching those most likely to convert into customers. As social media platforms offer powerful tools for precise targeting, a clear audience definition allows you to optimize your ad campaigns, increase click-through rates, and drive conversions. Defining your target audience is not just about speaking to the right people; it is about creating meaningful connections, optimizing resources, and achieving tangible business outcomes in the competitive world of social media marketing.

Creating Customer Personas

Creating customer personas is essential in developing a robust social media marketing strategy. A customer persona is a semi-fictional representation of your ideal customer based on market research and data analysis. It goes beyond generic demographics and delves into your potential customers' motivations, behaviors, preferences, and pain points. This process involves gathering insights from various sources, such as surveys, social media analytics, and customer feedback, to understand your target audience segments comprehensively. Each persona represents a distinct group of individuals with shared characteristics, allowing you to tailor your content and messaging to resonate more personally.

The significance of customer personas lies in their ability to guide your entire social media strategy. When you have a clear picture of your customers, you can craft content that addresses their needs and aspirations. From the tone of your posts to the choice of visuals, everything can be aligned with what resonates most with each persona. Customer personas also aid in the selection of appropriate platforms and engagement strategies. For instance, if one persona is more active on Instagram while another prefers LinkedIn, your plan can adapt accordingly. This targeted approach enhances your brand's authenticity and maximizes engagement and conversion rates. Customer personas serve as a unifying reference point for your entire team, aligning everyone toward a shared understanding of who you are trying to reach and how to do so effectively.

Ultimately, creating customer personas is a data-driven exercise that transforms generic demographics into vivid characters with distinct personalities, behaviors, and needs. By harnessing the power of these personas, you create a compass that steers your social media marketing efforts toward a more meaningful and impactful interaction with your audience.

Identifying Audience Pain Points and Desires

Identifying audience pain points and desires is pivotal to an effective social media marketing strategy. Pain points are the specific challenges, problems, or frustrations your target audience faces, while desires are the aspirations, goals, and dreams they seek to achieve. Understanding these emotional triggers provides insights into what motivates your audience, enabling you to tailor your content to address their needs and aspirations directly.

Identifying pain points and desires involves a combination of research and empathy. This entails actively listening to your audience through social media interactions, surveys, reviews, and comments. Dive into conversations related to your industry, monitor feedback on your products or services, and analyze the questions and concerns your audience raises. You can uncover the underlying motivations behind their behavior by studying their language, emotions, and pain points. This empathetic approach enables you to create resonating content and establishes a deeper connection.

The significance of identifying pain points and desires lies in its ability to position your brand as a solution provider. You establish trust and credibility when you address your audience's challenges and showcase how your offerings can alleviate their pain points or help them achieve their desires. Your content becomes a beacon of value, and your social media presence transforms into a platform that offers genuine solutions. By aligning your messaging with what truly matters to your audience, you tap into their emotional triggers, driving engagement, loyalty, and conversions. In the competitive realm of social media, understanding your audience's pain points and desires sets you apart by showing that you genuinely care and are attuned to their needs.

* * *

Key Takeaways:

- Defining your target audience involves considering demographics, psychographics, and other vital factors.
- Customer personas offer a detailed understanding of your ideal customers' motivations and preferences.
- Addressing audience pain points and desires in your content enhances engagement and connection.

Action Steps:

- Create detailed customer personas for each segment of your target audience.

- Conduct market research to uncover the pain points and desires that resonate with your audience.

2

Understanding Your Audience

Defining Your Target Audience

Successful social media marketing begins with understanding your target audience. Defining your target audience is the cornerstone of a successful social media marketing strategy. It identifies the people most likely to resonate with your brand, products, or services. This step is not just about broad demographics but about understanding your potential customers' deeper characteristics, behaviors, interests, and pain points. By delving into the specifics of your target audience, you gain insights that allow you to tailor your content, messaging, and engagement strategies precisely. This targeted approach ensures that your efforts resonate more profoundly, making your brand stand out in a sea of content. Whether creating compelling visuals, writing persuasive copy, or interacting with followers, clearly understanding your target audience allows you to connect personally, fostering trust and loyalty.

The benefits of defining your target audience extend beyond resonating with your customers – it also maximizes your return on investment. Resources are valuable, and targeting the right audience ensures you direct your efforts where they matter most. With a well-defined audience, you can allocate your budget and resources effectively, reaching those most likely to convert into customers. As social media platforms offer powerful tools for precise targeting, a clear audience definition allows you the ability to optimize your ad campaigns, increase click-through rates, and drive conversions. Defining your target audience is not just about speaking to the right people; it is about creating meaningful connections, optimizing resources, and achieving tangible business outcomes in the competitive world of social media marketing.

Creating Customer Personas

Creating customer personas is essential in developing a robust social media marketing strategy. A customer persona is a semi-fictional representation of your ideal customer based on market research and data analysis. It goes beyond generic demographics and delves into your potential customers' motivations, behaviors, preferences, and pain points. This process involves gathering insights from various sources, such as surveys, social media analytics, and customer feedback, to understand your target audience segments comprehensively. Each persona represents a distinct group of individuals with shared characteristics, allowing you to tailor your content and messaging to resonate more personally.

The significance of customer personas lies in their ability to guide your entire social media strategy. When you have a clear picture of your customers, you can craft content that addresses their needs and aspirations. From the tone of your posts to the choice of visuals, everything can be aligned with what resonates most with each persona. Customer personas also aid in the selection of appropriate platforms and engagement strategies. For instance, if one persona is more active on Instagram while another prefers LinkedIn, your strategy can adapt accordingly. This targeted approach enhances your brand's authenticity and maximizes engagement and conversion rates. Customer personas serve as a unifying reference point for your entire team, aligning everyone toward a shared understanding of who you are trying to reach and how to do so effectively.

Ultimately, creating customer personas is a data-driven exercise that transforms generic demographics into vivid characters with distinct personalities, behaviors, and needs. By harnessing the power of these personas, you create a compass that steers your social media marketing efforts toward a more meaningful and impactful interaction with your audience.

Identifying Audience Pain Points and Desires

Identifying audience pain points and desires is pivotal to constructing an effective social media marketing strategy. Pain points are the specific challenges, problems, or frustrations your target audience faces, while desires are the aspirations, goals, and dreams they seek to achieve. Understanding these emotional triggers provides insights into what motivates your audience, enabling you to tailor your content to address their needs and aspirations directly.

Identifying pain points and desires involves a combination of research and empathy. This entails actively listening to your audience through social media interactions, surveys, reviews, and comments. Dive into conversations related to your industry, monitor feedback on your products or services, and analyze the questions and concerns your audience raises. You can uncover their behavior's underlying motivations by studying their language, emotions, and pain points. This empathetic approach enables you to create resonating content and establishes a deeper connection.

The significance of identifying pain points and desires lies in its ability to position your brand as a solution provider. You establish trust and credibility when you address your audience's challenges and showcase how your offerings can alleviate their pain points or help them achieve their desires. Your content becomes a beacon of value, and your social media presence transforms into a platform that offers genuine solutions. By aligning your messaging with what truly matters to your audience, you tap into their emotional triggers, driving engagement, loyalty, and conversions. In the competitive realm of social media, understanding your audience's pain points and desires sets you apart by showing that you genuinely care and are attuned to their needs.

* * *

Key Takeaways:

- Defining your target audience involves considering demographics, psychographics, and other key factors.
- Customer personas offer a detailed understanding of your ideal customers' motivations and preferences.
- Addressing audience pain points and desires in your content enhances engagement and connection.

Action Steps:

- Create detailed customer personas for each segment of your target audience.
- Conduct market research to uncover the pain points and desires that resonate with your audience.

3

Choosing the Right Platforms

Defining Your Target Audience

Successful social media marketing begins with understanding your target audience. Defining your target audience is the cornerstone of a successful social media marketing strategy. It identifies the people most likely to resonate with your brand, products, or services. This step is about broad demographics and understanding your potential customers' deeper characteristics, behaviors, interests, and pain points. By delving into the specifics of your target audience, you gain insights that allow you to tailor your content, messaging, and engagement strategies precisely. This targeted approach ensures that your efforts resonate more profoundly, making your brand stand out in a sea of content. Whether creating compelling visuals, writing persuasive copy, or interacting with followers, clearly understanding your target audience allows you to connect personally, fostering trust and loyalty.

The benefits of defining your target audience extend beyond resonating with your customers – it also maximizes your return on investment. Resources are valuable, and targeting the right audience ensures you direct your efforts where they matter most. With a well-defined audience, you can allocate your budget and resources effectively, reaching those most likely to convert into customers. As social media platforms offer powerful tools for precise targeting, a clear audience definition allows you to optimize your ad campaigns, increase click-through rates, and drive conversions. Defining your target audience is not just about speaking to the right people; it is about creating meaningful connections, optimizing resources, and achieving tangible business outcomes in the competitive world of social media marketing.

Creating Customer Personas

Creating customer personas is essential in developing a robust social media marketing strategy. A customer persona is a semi-fictional representation of your ideal customer based on market research and data analysis. It goes beyond generic demographics and delves into your potential customers' motivations, behaviors, preferences, and pain points. This process involves gathering insights from various sources, such as surveys, social media analytics, and customer feedback, to understand your target audience segments comprehensively. Each persona represents a distinct group of individuals with shared characteristics, allowing you to tailor your content and messaging to resonate more personally.

The significance of customer personas lies in their ability to guide your entire social media strategy. When you have a clear picture of your customers, you can craft content that addresses their needs and aspirations. From the tone of your posts to the choice of visuals, everything can be aligned with what resonates most with each persona. Customer personas also aid in the selection of appropriate platforms and engagement strategies. For instance, if one persona is more active on Instagram while another prefers LinkedIn, your plan can adapt accordingly. This targeted approach enhances your brand's authenticity and maximizes engagement and conversion rates. Customer personas serve as a unifying reference point for your entire team, aligning everyone toward a shared understanding of who you are trying to reach and how to do so effectively.

Ultimately, creating customer personas is a data-driven exercise that transforms generic demographics into vivid characters with distinct personalities, behaviors, and needs. By harnessing the power of these personas, you create a compass that steers your social media marketing efforts toward a more meaningful and impactful interaction with your audience.

Identifying Audience Pain Points and Desires

Identifying audience pain points and desires is pivotal to an effective social media marketing strategy. Pain points are the specific challenges, problems, or frustrations your target audience faces, while desires are the aspirations, goals, and dreams they seek to achieve. Understanding these emotional triggers provides insights into what motivates your audience, enabling you to tailor your content to address their needs and aspirations directly.

Identifying pain points and desires involves a combination of research and empathy. This entails actively listening to your audience through social media interactions, surveys, reviews, and comments. Dive into conversations related to your industry, monitor feedback on your products or services, and analyze the questions and concerns your audience raises. You can uncover the underlying motivations behind their behavior by studying their language, emotions, and pain points. This empathetic approach enables you to create resonating content and establishes a deeper connection.

The significance of identifying pain points and desires lies in its ability to position your brand as a solution provider. You establish trust and credibility when you address your audience's challenges and showcase how your offerings can alleviate their pain points or help them achieve their desires. Your content becomes a beacon of value, and your social media presence transforms into a platform that offers genuine solutions. By aligning your messaging with what truly matters to your audience, you tap into their emotional triggers, driving engagement, loyalty, and conversions. In the competitive realm of social media, understanding your audience's pain points and desires sets you apart by showing that you genuinely care and are attuned to their needs.

* * *

Key Takeaways:

- Defining your target audience involves considering demographics, psychographics, and other vital factors.
- Customer personas offer a detailed understanding of your ideal customers' motivations and preferences.
- Addressing audience pain points and desires in your content enhances engagement and connection.

Action Steps:

- Create detailed customer personas for each segment of your target audience.

- Conduct market research to uncover the pain points and desires that resonate with your audience.

4

Crafting A Winning Strategy

Setting Clear Goals and Objectives

Setting clear goals and objectives is the foundation of a successful social media strategy. Without a well-defined roadmap, your efforts can become scattered and lack direction. Goals provide a purpose and a sense of direction, guiding your content creation, engagement strategies, and performance measurement. Start by outlining specific, measurable, achievable, relevant, and time-bound (SMART) goals. For example, if your goal is to increase brand awareness, your objective could be to achieve a 20% increase in brand mentions and shares on social media within the next six months. Clarity in your goals ensures everyone on your team understands the desired outcomes and can work collectively to achieve them.

The process of setting goals involves aligning them with your overall business objectives. What are you trying to achieve as a company? Are you aiming for higher sales, greater customer satisfaction, or expanded market reach? Once you've established these broader objectives, break them down into social media-specific goals contributing to your business's success. Additionally, consider the buyer's journey. Are you trying to create awareness, generate leads, or drive conversions? Different stages of the buyer's journey require different content and engagement strategies. By aligning your goals with the buyer's journey, you can create a cohesive strategy that guides your audience through each stage, from discovery to conversion. Setting clear goals and objectives sets the stage for a focused, strategic, and results-driven social media marketing campaign.

Defining Key Performance Indicators (KPIs)

Defining Key Performance Indicators (KPIs) is a pivotal step in measuring the effectiveness and impact of your social media strategy. KPIs are specific metrics that help you gauge whether your efforts align with your goals and objectives. With well-defined KPIs, it's easier to assess the success of your social media campaigns and make informed decisions for improvement. Start by aligning your KPIs with your goals. If your goal is to enhance brand awareness, relevant KPIs include metrics like reach, impressions, and brand mentions. For lead generation, KPIs focus on click-through rates, form submissions, and downloads. Choosing KPIs that reflect your goals ensures your measurements are directly tied to your desired outcomes.

The process of defining KPIs involves a blend of specificity and relevance. Avoid measuring everything for the sake of it; instead, select a handful of KPIs that truly reflect the impact you're seeking to achieve. Consider your target audience and their behavior. Which metrics give you insights into how well you're connecting with and engaging your audience? For instance, engagement metrics such as likes, comments, shares, and retweets can gauge audience interaction and sentiment. Keep in mind that different platforms may require different KPIs. For example, on Instagram, engagement metrics are more relevant, while on LinkedIn, you focus on click-through rates and lead conversions. Continual monitoring and adjustment of your KPIs are crucial as your strategy evolves. Regularly assess whether your chosen KPIs provide valuable insights and adjust them if needed to stay aligned with your evolving goals.

Incorporating KPIs into your social media strategy empowers you with data-driven insights that inform your decisions and strategy refinement. These measurable metrics help you understand what's working, what needs improvement, and where to allocate resources for the best outcomes. With a clear focus on relevant KPIs, you can measure progress, optimize tactics, and demonstrate the tangible impact of your social media efforts to stakeholders within your organization.

Creating a Content Calendar and Posting Schedule

Consistency is key in social media marketing. Creating a content calendar and posting schedule is fundamental to structure and consistency in your social media strategy. It ensures that your content efforts are well-organized, aligned with your goals, and optimized for engagement. A content calendar provides a visual overview of your upcoming content, allowing you to plan, avoid last-minute rushes, and maintain a cohesive brand voice. Start by outlining the types of content you want to create, such as blog posts, images, videos, or infographics. Then, assign specific topics, themes, and key messages to each piece of content. Consider the frequency of your posts and the best times to engage with your target audience on each platform.

Creating a content calendar involves mapping out your content strategy over a defined period, whether a week, a month, or even a quarter. Tools like spreadsheets, project management software, or specialized social media scheduling platforms can help you organize and visualize your content plan. Be sure to align your content with your marketing campaigns, product launches, and industry trends. This ensures that your content remains relevant and timely, increasing the likelihood of engagement and shares. Furthermore, establish a posting schedule that outlines when each piece of content will be published on each platform. Consistency is key; it trains your audience to expect and look forward to your content. Posting at optimal times when your audience is most active can also enhance your content's reach and impact.

Incorporating a content calendar and posting schedule into your social media strategy fosters efficiency, consistency, and strategic planning. It allows you to maintain a steady flow of relevant content, engage with your audience regularly, and optimize your content strategy based on data insights. By having a clear plan in place, you can focus on creating high-quality content that resonates with your audience and drives meaningful interactions, ultimately contributing to the success of your social media campaigns.

* * *

Key Takeaways:

- Clear goals and objectives are the foundation of an effective social media strategy.

- Defining KPIs helps measure progress and adapt strategies accordingly.
- A content calendar and posting schedule ensure consistent and organized social media activity.

Action Steps:

- Define specific SMART goals for your social media strategy.
- Identify relevant KPIs that align with your objectives.
- Create a content calendar that outlines your content plan and posting schedule.

5

Creating Compelling Content

Types of Content: Visual, Written, Video, etc.

Diversifying your content is essential for keeping your audience engaged, catering to different preferences, and effectively conveying your brand's message. Various types of content serve distinct purposes, enabling you to tell your brand story, showcase products or services, and connect with your audience on a deeper level. Visual content, such as images and videos, is particularly impactful in capturing attention and conveying information quickly. It could include product demonstrations, behind-the-scenes glimpses, user-generated content, and visually appealing graphics that align with your brand aesthetics. These visuals create an emotional connection and increase the shareability of your content, contributing to your brand's visibility.

Written content, including blog posts, articles, and captions, is equally important. It allows you to provide your audience with in-depth insights, thought leadership, and educational value. Blog posts can delve into industry trends, best practices, and solutions to your audience's pain points. This type of content positions your brand as an authority and resource in your field, fostering trust and credibility. Interactive content, such as polls, quizzes, and videos, invites engagement and participation. These types of content entertain and encourage your audience to share their opinions and preferences, providing you with valuable insights. Additionally, user-generated content, where your customers share their experiences with your brand, can be a powerful way to build authenticity and social proof. Sharing customer testimonials, reviews, and success stories humanizes your brand and showcases real-world benefits.

Combining content types keeps your social media strategy dynamic, engaging, and appealing to a broader range of audience preferences. Whether visually striking images, informative blog posts, interactive polls, or heartfelt user stories, each type of content contributes to a holistic brand experience and helps you achieve your social media goals more effectively.

Storytelling Techniques for Engagement

Storytelling is a potent tool for capturing your audience's attention, evoking emotions, and creating a memorable brand identity. Incorporating storytelling techniques into your social media strategy can foster a deeper connection with your audience and enhance engagement. Start by identifying your brand's unique narrative – the core values, mission, and the journey that led you to where you are today. Craft your content to reflect this narrative, whether it's through relatable anecdotes, origin stories, or personal experiences. This approach makes your brand more relatable and human, inviting your audience to connect emotionally.

A technique that resonates particularly well on social media is the "hero's journey." This narrative follows a protagonist's transformation through challenges, growth, and triumphs. Translate this concept to your brand by showcasing how your products or services can be the hero in your customers' stories, solving their problems and fulfilling their aspirations. Involve your audience in the journey by sharing user-generated content, testimonials, and success stories. Another effective technique is "behind-the-scenes" content. Take your audience on a journey into your workspace, production process, or company culture. This transparent and authentic approach humanizes your brand, building trust and transparency. Moreover, don't shy away from vulnerability. Sharing challenges, failures, and lessons learned humanizes your brand and makes your journey relatable and inspiring to your audience.

Incorporating storytelling techniques into your social media strategy transforms your content into a compelling narrative that resonates with your audience. You create a deeper connection beyond transactional interactions by conveying emotions, values, and relatable experiences. Whether it's the hero's journey, behind-the-scenes glimpses, or vulnerable storytelling, each technique invites engagement, encourages sharing, and solidifies your brand's position as a source of value and inspiration in your audience's lives.

Leveraging User-Generated Content

User-generated content (UGC) is a powerful resource that can significantly enhance your social media strategy. It involves content created by your customers, followers, or fans that showcases their experiences with your brand. Leveraging UGC saves you time on content creation, builds authenticity, and fosters a sense of community around your brand. Encourage your audience to share their photos, videos, reviews, and stories about your products or services. UGC is social proof, demonstrating real-world use and satisfaction with your offerings.

To effectively leverage UGC, establish clear guidelines for submission. Communicate what types of content you're looking for, the format, and any specific hashtags to use. Showcase UGC on your social media platforms, website, and email campaigns. This recognition rewards your loyal customers and encourages others to participate. Sharing UGC demonstrates that you value your customers' voices and experiences, strengthening the emotional connection between your brand and your audience.

Moreover, UGC creates a cycle of engagement. Users feel appreciated and more likely to continue engaging with your brand when they see their content featured. This can lead to a positive feedback loop of increased engagement and advocacy.

Incorporating user-generated content into your social media strategy transforms your customers into brand advocates and co-creators. Their authentic content serves as a testament to the value your brand provides. Through UGC, you are not just promoting products; you are sharing real stories and experiences that resonate with your audience on a personal level. This approach enhances engagement and builds a loyal community that actively participates in your brand's narrative, contributing to its ongoing success.

* * *

Key Takeaways:

- Utilize a variety of content types to engage different audience segments.

- Storytelling adds depth and emotion to your content, fostering more robust connections.
- User-generated content can enhance engagement and build community.

Action Steps:

- Identify which content types align best with your audience and goals.
- Experiment with storytelling techniques to enhance the emotional impact of your content.
- Develop strategies for encouraging user-generated content from your audience.

6

Building an Engaged Community

Best Practices for Community Management

Community management nurtures and engages with your social media audience to build a loyal and active community around your brand. It is about fostering meaningful interactions, providing exceptional customer support, and creating a positive online environment. One essential practice is to be responsive. Monitor your social media platforms regularly for comments, messages, and mentions. Promptly respond to inquiries, feedback, and even criticism. Acknowledging every positive or negative interaction demonstrates that you value your audience's engagement and opinions. Responding with empathy and professionalism can turn negative experiences into positive ones and showcase your commitment to customer satisfaction.

Listening is another essential practice. Pay attention to the conversations happening around your brand, industry, and related topics. Actively participate in discussions, share relevant insights, and answer questions even if they're not directly associated with your products. This positions your brand as a valuable resource and a trusted authority in your field. Encourage user-generated content and engage with it. Showcase user posts, comments, and reviews that reflect positively on your brand. Doing so creates a sense of community ownership and fosters an environment where users feel appreciated for their contributions.

Another crucial practice is setting clear guidelines for engagement. Establish a tone of voice and style that aligns with your brand's identity. This consistency ensures that your interactions feel authentic and resonate with your audience. Be respectful and empathetic, and avoid confrontational responses. Additionally, be proactive in addressing issues. Monitor trends, identify potential conflicts, and respond before they escalate. Transparency and openness are key; if mistakes happen, acknowledge them and provide solutions. Remember, community management is not just about solving problems; it is about building relationships and turning your audience into brand advocates who passionately support and promote your offerings.

Incorporating these best practices into your community management approach helps cultivate an engaged and loyal following. Treating your audience as a valued community creates an environment where users feel heard, appreciated, and excited to interact with your brand. Effective community management can increase brand loyalty, positive word-of-mouth, and a thriving online ecosystem that amplifies your brand's impact.

Techniques for Increasing Engagement

Increasing engagement on social media requires a strategic approach that encourages meaningful interactions and fosters a sense of community around your brand. One effective technique is to create interactive content. Polls, quizzes, contests, and challenges invite participation and encourage users to share their opinions or experiences. These types of posts not only generate higher engagement rates but also provide valuable insights into your audience's preferences and interests. You build a two-way conversation beyond simple likes and shares by involving your audience in decision-making or fun activities.

Leveraging visual content is another powerful technique. Images and videos naturally capture attention and elicit emotional responses. Infographics can simplify complex information, while videos can tell compelling stories. Live streams and behind-the-scenes videos authentically peek into your brand's world. Utilize storytelling within your visuals to connect with your audience personally.

Additionally, encourage user-generated content (UGC). Prompt your audience to share their experiences, photos, and stories about your brand. Not only does this foster a sense of belonging, but it also provides you with a continuous stream of authentic content. Users feel acknowledged and valued when you feature UGC, motivating them to engage with your brand.

By implementing these techniques, you create an environment that encourages active participation and genuine connections on your social media platforms. Consistently offering interactive, visually appealing, and user-centric content transforms passive followers into engaged community members who eagerly interact with your brand, share their experiences, and contribute to your online presence.

Handling Negative Feedback and Customer Service

Handling negative feedback and providing exceptional customer service on social media is crucial to maintaining a positive brand image and building trust with your audience. When negative comments or reviews arise, respond promptly and professionally. Avoid deleting negative comments, as this can escalate the situation. Instead, address the issue publicly and express your commitment to resolving it. Maintain a calm and empathetic tone, acknowledging the customer's concern and showing that you value their feedback. Offer a solution or invite the customer to contact you privately to address the matter further. This transparent approach demonstrates your willingness to rectify issues and showcases your commitment to open communication.

For more complex issues, guide the conversation to direct messaging or email to ensure a thorough resolution. Customer service on social media should mirror the service customers receive through traditional channels. Aim to exceed expectations; go the extra mile to resolve the issue and show goodwill. Keep in mind that other users are watching how you handle negative feedback. Responding professionally and effectively can turn a negative experience into a positive impression and even win back disgruntled customers. Remember that not all negative feedback is terrible; it provides valuable insights into areas for improvement, helping you refine your products or services.

Incorporating a responsive and empathetic approach to negative feedback and customer service on social media can turn challenging situations into growth and brand loyalty opportunities. By addressing concerns publicly, offering solutions, and demonstrating your commitment to customer satisfaction, you are resolving individual issues and building a reputation for transparency, responsiveness, and exceptional service. These interactions contribute to a positive customer experience that resonates with your entire audience, creating a foundation of trust and authenticity around your brand.

* * *

Key Takeaways:

- Effective community management builds a loyal and engaged audience.
- Engagement techniques encourage interactions and create a dynamic community.
- Addressing negative feedback professionally can mitigate its impact on your brand.

Action Steps:

- Develop a community management strategy that outlines how you'll engage with your audience.
- Experiment with engagement techniques to gauge their impact on interaction levels.
- Prepare guidelines for addressing negative feedback and turning it into positive interactions.

7

Mastering Hashtags and Trends

Utilizing Hashtags for Visibility

Utilizing hashtags effectively can significantly enhance the visibility of your social media content and expand your reach to a broader audience. Hashtags serve as digital signposts, categorizing your posts and making them discoverable by users interested in similar topics. Research and choose hashtags relevant to your content and aligning with your target audience's interests. Consider both popular and niche hashtags that are commonly used within your industry. Including relevant hashtags in your posts increases the likelihood of your content appearing in search results and trending conversations.

However, it's important to use hashtags strategically and not to overload your posts with too many. Aim for a balance between specificity and broad appeal. Using too many hashtags can appear spammy and may dilute the impact of your message. A concise list of 3 to 5 well-chosen hashtags is generally effective on platforms like Instagram and Twitter. Remember that your goal is connecting with genuinely interested users in your content. Engage with the communities around these hashtags by interacting with posts, liking, commenting, and sharing. This increases your visibility and positions you as an active participant in relevant conversations.

By incorporating relevant and well-chosen hashtags into your social media content, you are harnessing a powerful tool to increase your content's discoverability and reach. Practical hashtag usage helps you tap into existing conversations, join relevant trends, and engage with a broader audience interested in the topics you are addressing. This visibility-building technique is a valuable strategy to enhance the impact of your social media efforts.

Participating in Trending Topics and Challenges

Participating in trending topics and challenges is a dynamic way to keep your social media strategy fresh, relevant, and engaging. Trending topics are conversations and hashtags that are currently popular and widely discussed on social media platforms. By joining these conversations, you align your brand with current events and tap into existing user engagement. When a relevant topic is trending, create content that contributes to the conversation while showcasing your brand's perspective. Be authentic and ensure your contribution adds value to the discussion. This strategy increases your visibility and positions your brand as actively engaged and in touch with current trends.

On the other hand, challenges are specific content prompts that encourage users to participate by creating their own versions of the challenge. Challenges often go viral, and by creating or participating in one, you leverage the power of user-generated content and increase engagement. Participating in challenges showcases your brand's fun and human side while encouraging your audience to get involved. Craft content that aligns with your brand's identity and the challenge theme. Whether it is a dance challenge, a creative task, or a shared experience, ensure your content aligns with your brand values and resonates with your target audience.

Engaging with trending topics and challenges transforms your social media strategy into an active and responsive presence. By staying current and participating in relevant conversations, you position your brand as a thought leader and an active participant in the online community. This approach creates opportunities for increased engagement, higher visibility, and even the potential to go viral. Remember to maintain authenticity and relevance in all your interactions to make the most of this strategy.

* * *

Key Takeaways:

- Hashtags enhance the discoverability of your content across platforms.
- Participating in trending topics and challenges can boost engagement and visibility.

Action Steps:

- Research and compile a list of relevant hashtags for your industry and niche.
- Strategically integrate trending topics and challenges into your content plan.

8

Influencer Collaboration

Identifying and Partnering with Influencers

Identifying and partnering with influencers can be a game-changing strategy to amplify your brand's reach, credibility, and engagement. Influencers are individuals with a significant and engaged following on social media platforms. Collaborating with them allows you to tap into their established audience, gaining access to potential customers who trust their recommendations. Begin by researching influencers within your industry or niche. Look for those whose values, content style, and target audience align with your brand. Evaluate their engagement rates, authenticity, and relevance to ensure a genuine connection with your audience.

When partnering with influencers, focus on building authentic relationships. Reach out to influencers whose content resonates with your brand's message and mission. Tailor your approach to their preferences and show genuine interest in their content. When proposing a collaboration, emphasize the mutual benefits – how your product or service aligns with their interests and how their endorsement can bring value to their followers. Be transparent about compensation or incentives, and discuss the terms of the partnership clearly to avoid misunderstandings.

Influencer partnerships inject fresh energy into your social media strategy, exposing your brand to new audiences and boosting credibility through trusted endorsements. By identifying influencers whose values align with your brand and fostering genuine relationships, you create an environment where mutual authenticity resonates with the influencer's audience and existing customers. This strategic alliance can increase engagement, broader brand exposure, and an enhanced reputation within your target market.

Structuring Successful Influencer Campaigns

Structuring successful influencer campaigns involves careful planning, clear communication, and focusing on mutual benefits. Begin by defining your campaign's objectives – increasing brand awareness, driving sales, or launching a new product. Based on your goals, identify influencers whose audience aligns with your target demographic. Once you have selected influencers, establish the campaign's key messages and guidelines. Provide them with creative freedom while ensuring your brand's messaging remains consistent.

The content format should align with the influencer's strengths and the platform's features. Whether it's Instagram posts, YouTube videos, or Twitter threads, ensure the content feels natural and genuine. Collaborate on a content calendar and posting schedule, and outline how each content contributes to the overall campaign narrative. Transparency is critical; communicate compensation, whether monetary, products, or a combination of both. Additionally, monitor and measure the campaign's performance using relevant metrics: track engagement, reach, click-through rates, and conversions to assess the campaign's effectiveness. Regular communication with influencers throughout the campaign ensures that expectations are met and adjustments can be made in real-time.

Structuring influencer campaigns with precision and open communication ensures your brand's message is effectively communicated to a broader audience through trusted advocates. You create a symbiotic relationship that benefits both parties by aligning campaign goals, content, and compensation with the influencers' values and strengths. A well-executed influencer campaign enhances your brand's visibility, credibility, and engagement, propelling your social media strategy to new heights of success.

* * *

Key Takeaways:

- Influencer collaborations can extend your brand's reach and credibility.
- Successful influencer campaigns require strategic planning and clear objectives.

Action Steps:

- Research and compile a list of potential influencers in your industry.
- Outline the key components of a successful influencer campaign, including goals and content guidelines.

9

Paid Social Advertising

Introduction to Social Media Advertising

Social media advertising is a powerful digital marketing strategy that allows businesses to promote their products, services, or brands to a highly targeted audience across various social media platforms. Unlike organic posts, social media ads are paid content that appears in users' feeds, timelines, or other designated ad spaces. This form of advertising enables brands to reach specific demographics, interests, and behaviors and even retarget individuals who have previously engaged with their content or visited their website.

The foundation of successful social media advertising lies in understanding your target audience and platform capabilities. Start by defining your campaign objectives – driving website traffic, generating leads, increasing sales, or building brand awareness. Choose the social media platforms that align with your audience's demographics and preferences. Facebook, Instagram, Twitter, LinkedIn, and Pinterest offer versatile advertising options with various formats, such as image ads, video ads, carousel ads, and sponsored posts. Each platform provides unique targeting tools, allowing you to pinpoint your desired audience based on age, location, interests, behaviors, and more.

As you delve into social media advertising, allocating a budget, setting bid strategies, and creating compelling ad content that resonates with your audience is essential. Ad copy and visuals should be engaging, concise, and aligned with your brand identity. Utilize eye-catching visuals and concise messaging to capture users' attention in the crowded digital landscape. Regularly monitor your ad performance and adjust your strategies based on key metrics such as click-through rates, conversions, and return on ad spend. By harnessing the power of social media advertising, businesses can strategically reach and engage their target audience, drive desired actions, and achieve their marketing goals in a measurable and impactful way.

Targeting Options and Ad Formats

Social media advertising offers a wide array of targeting options and ad formats that empower businesses to connect with their ideal audience in a highly personalized manner. The success of your campaigns hinges on selecting the right combination of targeting and ad formats that resonate with your audience's preferences and behaviors.

Targeting options in social media advertising are remarkably sophisticated. Platforms like Facebook, Instagram, and LinkedIn allow you to narrow down your audience based on demographics such as age, gender, location, education, and job title. Moreover, interests and behaviors can be leveraged for precise targeting. You can reach users interested in specific hobbies, industries, brands, or even those who have engaged with similar content. Custom audience targeting is another potent tool that lets you upload lists of existing customers or website visitors to create highly relevant ad campaigns. Lookalike audiences take this a step further by identifying users who share characteristics with your existing customers, expanding your reach to potential new customers with similar profiles.

Complementing these targeting options are diverse ad formats that cater to different goals and audience preferences. Image ads offer visually engaging content, while video ads bring your brand story to life. Carousel ads allow you to showcase multiple products or features in a single ad unit, fostering deeper engagement. Slideshow ads offer dynamic motion with fewer resources than video, making them ideal for captivating audiences. Lead generation ads simplify capturing user information, while collection ads combine imagery and a fullscreen experience to showcase products. Each ad format serves a unique purpose, and selecting the appropriate one depends on your campaign objectives and the preferences of your target audience.

Incorporating the right targeting options and ad formats in your social media advertising campaigns maximizes your impact by ensuring that your content reaches the right people in a format they find appealing. By effectively leveraging the tools at your disposal, you can create campaigns that capture attention and drive desired actions, ultimately contributing to your brand's growth and success.

Budgeting and Measuring ROI

Budgeting is a critical aspect of social media advertising that requires careful consideration to allocate resources effectively and achieve optimal results. Determining your advertising budget involves evaluating your overall marketing goals, the platforms you'll be using, and the specific objectives of each campaign. Start by defining clear objectives, whether generating leads, increasing sales, or raising brand awareness. Consider your campaigns' lifespan, whether short-term promotions or ongoing efforts. Allocate your budget based on your target audience size, platform costs, and the level of competition in your industry. Testing and experimentation are essential; start with a manageable budget and refine it as you gather insights about what works best for your brand.

Measuring your social media advertising campaigns' return on investment (ROI) is crucial to assessing their effectiveness and guiding future decisions. ROI is calculated by comparing the revenue generated from your campaigns against the cost of running those campaigns. Platforms like Facebook and Instagram provide robust analytics tools that track key metrics such as clicks, impressions, conversions, and engagement. Analyzing these metrics lets you determine which campaigns deliver the best results and adjust your strategies accordingly. For example, if a particular campaign has a high click-through rate but a low conversion rate, you might need to optimize your landing page or refine your targeting.

Effective budgeting and ROI measurement provide valuable insights into the impact of your social media advertising efforts. By allocating resources strategically and continually analyzing your results, you can optimize your campaigns for maximum efficiency and success. As you fine-tune your strategies based on measurable data, you are better positioned to achieve your marketing objectives and ensure that every dollar invested in social media advertising generates a meaningful return.

* * *

Key Takeaways:

- Paid social advertising offers targeted reach and specific campaign goals.
- Targeting options, ad formats, and tracking ROI are essential for effective campaigns.

Action Steps:

- Research different social media advertising platforms and their capabilities.
- Define your target audience and select appropriate ad formats for your campaign.
- Establish a budget and develop a plan for tracking and measuring ROI.

10

Analyzing and Optimizing

Tools for Social Media Analytics

Analytics tools are essential for gaining valuable insights into your performance, understanding audience behavior, and refining your strategy. These tools provide a comprehensive view of your social media efforts, helping you measure the impact of your content, identify trends, and make data-driven decisions.

Platform-native analytics tools, such as those provided by Facebook Insights, Twitter Analytics, and Instagram Insights, offer insights specific to each platform. They provide metrics like engagement rates, reach, impressions, and follower demographics. These tools are valuable for understanding how your content resonates with your audience on each platform. However, for a more holistic view of your overall social media strategy, third-party social media management tools come into play.

Third-party tools like Hootsuite, Buffer, Sprout Social, and Google Analytics provide centralized dashboards that allow you to track multiple platforms in one place. These tools offer a deeper analysis of your performance, allowing you to compare the effectiveness of different platforms and campaigns. They often provide more advanced features like competitor analysis, sentiment tracking, and custom reporting. Additionally, these tools help schedule and automate posts, which can streamline your content creation process.

Using social media analytics tools, you can refine your strategy, optimize your content, and measure your ROI accurately. Whether using platform-native insights or third-party management tools, harnessing data-driven insights is critical to staying competitive and continuously improving your social media presence.

Interpreting Data to Refine Strategy

Interpreting data is a pivotal step in refining your social media strategy, as it empowers you to make informed decisions that drive engagement, conversions, and overall growth. Identify key performance indicators (KPIs) that align with your campaign objectives. These KPIs could include click-through rates, conversion rates, engagement rates, and follower growth. By tracking these metrics over time, you can assess the effectiveness of your efforts and identify trends.

Regularly analyze your data to uncover insights. Look for patterns in content performance, such as the posts that generate the most engagement or when your audience is most active. Use this information to tailor your content strategy, posting schedules, and ad targeting. For example, if you notice that video content consistently receives higher engagement, consider creating more videos to resonate with your audience.

A/B testing is a powerful technique for interpreting data. Experiment with different variables, such as post formats, headlines, visuals, or posting times, to determine what resonates best with your audience. Compare the results of these tests to refine your strategy and optimize your content for maximum impact. Additionally, keep an eye on your competitors and industry trends. By analyzing their performance, you can gain insights into what works in your industry and adapt your approach accordingly.

Incorporating data interpretation into your social media strategy ensures you are not just relying on assumptions but making decisions based on tangible evidence. By leveraging insights from your analytics, you can continually refine your content, posting schedule, and overall approach to achieve better engagement, reach, and results. This data-driven approach is essential for staying agile in the ever-evolving landscape of social media marketing.

A/B Testing and Continuous Improvement

A/B testing, or split testing, is a systematic approach to improving your social media strategy by comparing two versions of a content element to determine which one performs better. This technique involves creating two variations of a post, ad, or other content, with a single variable changed between them. This variable could be the headline, image, call-to-action, or posting time. By presenting these variations to different segments of your audience and measuring the performance of each, you can gather valuable insights into what resonates best with your audience.

A/B testing helps you make data-driven decisions rather than relying on assumptions. It enables you to optimize your content based on real-world performance rather than guesswork. For instance, if you are unsure whether a humorous or educational tone will resonate better with your audience, A/B testing allows you to gather evidence and refine your messaging accordingly. This process of testing and analyzing helps you fine-tune your strategies over time and uncover the most effective approaches for engaging your audience and achieving your goals.

Continuous improvement is a fundamental philosophy that should underpin your social media strategy. Building on the insights gained from A/B testing and data interpretation, this approach involves an ongoing cycle of testing, analyzing, and adapting. By consistently seeking opportunities for enhancement, you can refine your content, optimize your posting schedule, and align your strategies with the evolving preferences of your audience. The digital landscape is dynamic, and what works today might not work tomorrow. Embracing continuous improvement ensures that your social media strategy remains relevant and effective in the face of changing trends and audience behaviors.

Incorporating A/B testing and a commitment to continuous improvement into your social media strategy fosters a culture of innovation and data-driven decision-making. You systematically refine your tactics based on measurable results to position your brand for sustained growth and engagement. This approach empowers you to adapt to shifts in audience behavior, platform algorithms, and industry trends, ultimately increasing your chances of success in the ever-evolving world of social media marketing.

* * *

Key Takeaways:

- Analytics tools provide insights into social media performance and audience behavior.

- Data interpretation informs strategy refinement and optimization.
- A/B testing and continuous improvement are crucial for staying ahead in social media marketing.

Action Steps:

- Explore analytics tools available for each social media platform you use.
- Analyze data to identify successful content and areas for improvement.
- Plan and execute A/B tests to optimize your social media efforts.

11

Staying Ahead of Trends

Staying Abreast of Social Media Trends

Social media platforms are dynamic ecosystems that undergo frequent changes in algorithms, user behavior, and features. Awareness of and adapting to these trends allows businesses to remain relevant, connect with their audience effectively, and harness emerging opportunities.

Maintaining visibility and engagement is paramount when staying updated on social media trends. Platforms regularly introduce or modify new features to cater to evolving user preferences. Informed businesses can leverage these features strategically, creating content that aligns with current trends and capturing the attention of their target audience. For example, the rise of short-form videos on platforms like TikTok and Instagram Reels has shifted the content landscape, prompting brands to explore creative ways to convey their messages in concise and engaging formats.

Social media trends often reflect broader cultural shifts and societal interests. Understanding these trends allows businesses to align their messaging with the zeitgeist, fostering a sense of relatability and resonance with their audience. This enhances brand authenticity and positions the business as a forward-thinking entity that understands and responds to its customers' evolving needs and preferences.

Staying abreast of social media trends is crucial for maintaining a competitive edge. The digital landscape is highly competitive, and businesses proactively embracing new trends are better positioned to stand out and differentiate themselves from competitors. Whether adopting emerging content formats, participating in prevalent challenges, or utilizing the latest advertising features, businesses that quickly adapt can gain a first-mover advantage, capturing audiences' attention and staying ahead in their respective industries.

Staying updated on social media trends is a strategic imperative for businesses aiming to thrive in the digital age. It enables them to optimize their content strategies, connect with their audience on a deeper level, and remain competitive in a constantly evolving online landscape. By embracing trends, businesses enhance their visibility and engagement and demonstrate their agility and responsiveness to the ever-changing dynamics of the digital world.

Adapting to Algorithm Changes

Social media algorithms govern the visibility and reach of content, and they undergo frequent modifications as platforms strive to enhance user experience and engagement. Understanding and responding to these changes is crucial for businesses to ensure their content remains discoverable and effectively reaches their target audience.

One primary importance of adapting to algorithm changes lies in maximizing content visibility. Social media algorithms dictate the order in which content appears on users' feeds, considering factors such as relevance, engagement, and timeliness. When algorithms change, the visibility of content can be affected. Adapting to these changes allows businesses to align their content strategies with the updated criteria, ensuring their posts are prioritized and reach a wider audience. For example, if a platform shifts towards favoring video content, businesses need to adjust their strategy to incorporate more video-based posts to maintain optimal visibility.

Adapting to algorithm changes is essential for sustaining engagement levels. Algorithms often prioritize content that receives higher levels of engagement, such as likes, comments, and shares. As platforms refine their algorithms to enhance user satisfaction, businesses must agilely tailor their content to encourage meaningful interactions. This could involve crafting content that sparks discussions, encourages user participation, or aligns with trending topics. By staying attuned to algorithmic adjustments, businesses can ensure their content remains engaging and resonant with their audience.

Adapting to algorithm changes is also instrumental in optimizing advertising efforts. Many social media platforms use algorithms to determine which ads are shown to specific users. Understanding these algorithms enables businesses to refine their targeting strategies, ensuring their ads are displayed to the most relevant audience segments. For instance, if a platform introduces new targeting options or adjusts its ad-ranking criteria, businesses must adapt their advertising strategies to leverage these changes effectively.

Adapting to algorithm changes is a fundamental aspect of navigating the dynamic landscape of social media. It ensures businesses can maintain content visibility, sustain engagement levels, and optimize their advertising efforts. By staying informed and responsive to algorithmic updates, companies can position themselves for success in a highly competitive digital environment, where the ability to adapt to change is critical to achieving long-term growth and relevance.

Future Trends and Predictions

While predicting the future of social media is always dynamic, several trends are expected to shape the landscape in the coming years. These trends can redefine how businesses and individuals engage with social platforms, influencing content creation, communication strategies, and overall digital experiences.

Rise of Augmented Reality (AR) and Virtual Reality (VR): The integration of AR and VR technologies is anticipated to revolutionize social media interactions. Platforms may increasingly adopt AR filters, effects, and immersive experiences, providing users with more engaging and interactive content. Virtual events and spaces could become more commonplace, changing how people connect online.

Ephemeral Content Evolution: The popularity of short content, like Stories on platforms such as Instagram and Snapchat, is expected to continue growing. Short-lived, authentic content appeals to users, and businesses will likely leverage this trend for more spontaneous and real-time engagement, fostering a sense of urgency and exclusivity.

Increased Emphasis on Privacy and Data Protection: As privacy and data security concerns rise, social media platforms will likely enhance their privacy features and give users more control over their personal information. Messaging apps with end-to-end encryption may become even more prevalent, offering secure communication channels.

Continued Growth of Video Content: Video content consumption will dominate social media further. Short-form videos, live streams, and interactive video features are expected to gain momentum. Businesses will need to invest in creating compelling video content to capture the attention of their audiences effectively.

Voice and Audio Content: The popularity of voice-based platforms and audio content is rising. Podcasts, audio, and social networks are gaining traction, presenting new opportunities for content creators and businesses to connect with audiences more intimately and conveniently.

Niche and Specialized Platforms: While significant platforms continue to thrive, niche and specialized platforms catering to specific interests or demographics may gain prominence. Users seeking more focused and authentic communities might migrate towards platforms that align closely with their passions.

Artificial Intelligence (AI) Integration: AI-driven features, such as chatbots, personalized content recommendations, and advanced analytics, are likely to become more sophisticated. AI can enhance user experiences, streamline communication, and help businesses gain deeper insights into their audience's preferences.

Sustainability and Social Responsibility: Social media users increasingly value brands and platforms, prioritizing sustainability and social responsibility. Companies incorporating eco-friendly practices and contributing positively to societal issues will likely garner greater support and engagement.

Global Influencer Market: The influencer marketing landscape is expected to expand globally, with micro-influencers gaining prominence. Brands may focus on more localized and authentic influencer collaborations to resonate with specific audiences.

Blockchain for Transparency: Blockchain technology may find applications in social media for enhanced transparency, secure transactions, and content authenticity. Decentralized social platforms could emerge, giving users greater control over their data and content.

While these predictions offer insights into potential trends, the landscape remains dynamic and subject to unexpected shifts. Adapting to emerging trends will be key for businesses and content creators looking to stay ahead in the evolving world of social media.

* * *

Key Takeaways:

- Staying informed about social media trends is crucial for maintaining relevance.
- Adapting to algorithm changes helps maintain content visibility.
- Predicting future trends enables strategic preparation for shifts in the industry.

Action Steps:

- Follow reputable sources for social media news and updates.
- Monitor platform changes and adjust your strategy accordingly.
- Consider the future trends and brainstorm ways to integrate them into your strategy.

12

Case Studies and Success Stories

Real-World Examples of Social Media Success

Nike's "Dream Crazy" Campaign: Nike's "Dream Crazy" campaign featuring Colin Kaepernick is a powerful example of leveraging social issues for brand messaging. Despite initial controversy, the campaign received widespread attention and praise for its bold stance on social justice. The brand effectively utilized social media platforms to share the campaign video, sparking conversations and generating significant engagement. In this instance, Nike's social media success showcased the impact of aligning with social causes that resonate with the audience, contributing to increased brand visibility and positive sentiment.

Airbnb's #WeAccept Campaign: In response to the global refugee crisis, Airbnb launched the #WeAccept campaign in 2017. The campaign aimed to promote inclusivity and acceptance by showcasing the stories of Airbnb hosts opening their homes to refugees and those in need. The company utilized various social media platforms to share impactful stories and encourage users to pledge their support. The campaign's success was evident in the widespread sharing of its content, the adoption of the #WeAccept hashtag, and the positive sentiment generated across social media, contributing to Airbnb's reputation as a socially responsible brand.

Wendy's Twitter Roasts: Wendy's, a fast-food chain, gained social media acclaim for its witty interactions on Twitter. The brand engaged with users through clever comebacks and playful roasts, creating a distinct and memorable online persona. Wendy's social media success is a testament to the effectiveness of injecting humor and personality into brand communication. The approach garnered significant attention, increased engagement, and even led to media coverage, showcasing how a unique social media strategy can set a brand apart in a crowded market.

Dove's Real Beauty Campaign: Dove's Real Beauty Campaign is a prime example of how authenticity and inclusivity can resonate with audiences. The campaign challenged conventional beauty standards by featuring women of diverse body shapes, sizes, and ethnicities. Social media played a crucial role in sharing the campaign's messages, with the hashtag #RealBeauty becoming a platform for users to express their support and share personal stories. The campaign's success lies in connecting emotionally with the audience, sparking a broader societal conversation about beauty norms.

Oreo's Dunk in the Dark: During the 2013 Super Bowl, when the lights went out in the stadium, Oreo seized the moment with a timely and clever tweet that read, "Power out? No problem. You can still dunk in the dark." The tweet quickly went viral, showcasing the real-time marketing potential of social media. Oreo's quick and creative response capitalized on a real-world event and demonstrated the brand's agility and ability to engage with its audience in a fun and relevant way.

These real-world examples highlight the diverse approaches to social media success, emphasizing the importance of authenticity, creativity, and the strategic alignment of brand messages with societal conversations. Each case underscores the impact of effectively leveraging social media platforms to connect with audiences, drive engagement, and establish a memorable brand presence.

Lessons Learned from Various Industries

Retail and E-Commerce:

Lessons from Amazon: Amazon's success in the retail and e-commerce industry is marked by its strategic use of social media to enhance customer experiences. The key lesson here is leveraging social media as a customer service tool. Amazon employs platforms like Twitter to promptly respond to customer queries, address concerns, and provide real-time assistance. This exemplifies the significance of using social media for marketing, promoting, and maintaining strong customer relationships.

Technology:

Lessons from Apple: Apple's social media success is characterized by its ability to generate buzz and anticipation around product launches. The lesson here is creating a sense of exclusivity and excitement. By strategically revealing product details, teasers, and behind-the-scenes content on social media platforms, Apple builds anticipation, engages its audience, and ensures high interest before a product even hits the market. This underscores the importance of storytelling and creating a narrative around brand events to capture the audience's attention.

Hospitality:

Lessons from Marriott: In the hospitality industry, Marriott International has excelled in using social media to create a sense of community among its guests. Marriott's Bonvoy loyalty program is promoted through social media channels, fostering engagement and providing exclusive content to members. The lesson here is the power of community-building and personalized experiences. By recognizing and rewarding customer loyalty through social media platforms, Marriott establishes a connection beyond transactions, leading to increased brand advocacy and repeat business.

Healthcare:

Lessons from Mayo Clinic: Mayo Clinic's success in the healthcare industry is attributed to its commitment to providing reliable and informative content on social media. The lesson learned is the importance of establishing credibility and trust. Mayo Clinic utilizes platforms like YouTube, Twitter, and Facebook to share medical advice, research updates, and patient stories. By positioning itself as a reliable source of information, Mayo Clinic demonstrates the value of building trust through educational and authoritative content in industries where credibility is paramount.

Automotive:

Lessons from Tesla: Tesla's social media success in the automotive industry is driven by its emphasis on user-generated content and community engagement. The lesson here is the effectiveness of fostering a passionate community around a brand. Tesla encourages its customers to share their experiences, photos, and feedback on social media platforms, creating a strong community of advocates. This highlights the importance of empowering your audience to be brand ambassadors, contributing to a positive brand image, and attracting a wider audience.

These lessons from various industries emphasize the versatility of social media strategies. Whether using social media for customer service, creating anticipation through exclusive content, building a sense of community, establishing credibility, or encouraging user-generated content, businesses can tailor their approaches based on industry-specific dynamics to achieve social media success.

* * *

Key Takeaways:

- Case studies offer practical insights into successful social media campaigns.
- Lessons from various industries can be adapted to your specific context.

Action Steps:

- Analyze the strategies and tactics used in the showcased case studies.
- Identify key takeaways and consider how they can be applied to your social media efforts.

13

Crafting Your Comprehensive Social Media Plan

As you have journeyed through the pages of this book, you have gained valuable insights into the intricacies of social media strategy. Now, it is time to synthesize this knowledge into a concrete plan to propel your brand toward success in the digital realm. This chapter will guide you through a step-by-step process to craft your comprehensive social media plan, ensuring that every element of your strategy is aligned, purposeful, and primed for success.

Define Your Objectives and Goals

Begin by clearly defining the objectives you aim to achieve through your social media efforts. Are you looking to increase brand awareness, drive website traffic, generate leads, or boost sales? Each objective should be specific, measurable, achievable, relevant, and time-bound (SMART). Once you have established your objectives, set corresponding goals that will serve as benchmarks for success.

Understand Your Audience

Next, delve deep into understanding your target audience. Develop detailed audience personas that encapsulate your ideal customer's demographics, psychographics, preferences, pain points, and behaviors. By empathizing with your audience and gaining insights into their needs and desires, you will be better equipped to tailor your content and engagement strategies to resonate with them authentically.

Craft Compelling Content

With a clear understanding of your objectives and audience, it is time to create compelling content that captivates and resonates. Develop a content strategy encompassing diverse formats, including articles, videos, infographics, podcasts, and interactive posts. Align your content with your brand voice, values, and messaging, ensuring consistency across all platforms.

Choose the Right Platforms

Select the social media platforms that align with your objectives, audience demographics, and content strategy. Whether it is Facebook, Instagram, Twitter, LinkedIn, YouTube, or emerging platforms like TikTok, prioritize quality over quantity. Focus your efforts on platforms where your audience is most active and where your content will perform best.

Develop Engagement Strategies

Engagement is the lifeblood of social media success. Develop strategies to foster meaningful interactions with your audience, including responding to comments, messages, and mentions promptly, initiating conversations, and actively participating in relevant communities and discussions. Cultivate a community-centric approach that prioritizes building relationships and nurturing connections.

Set Key Performance Indicators (KPIs) and Metrics

Establish key performance indicators (KPIs) that align with your objectives and goals. Whether it is measuring engagement rates, website traffic, lead generation, or conversion metrics, select KPIs that provide actionable insights into the performance of your social media efforts. Utilize social media analytics tools to track and analyze relevant metrics, refining your strategy based on data-driven insights.

Create a Content Calendar and Posting Schedule

Develop a content calendar that outlines the types of content you will share, along with the frequency and timing of your posts. Consistency is key, so establish a posting schedule that ensures a steady content stream across your chosen platforms. Use scheduling tools to streamline the content creation and publishing process, allowing you to maintain a consistent presence without sacrificing quality.

Implement, Monitor, and Adapt

Finally, it is time to implement your social media plan, monitoring its performance closely and adapting as necessary. Regularly review your KPIs and analytics data, identifying trends, successes, and areas for improvement. Be agile and responsive, adjusting your strategy based on changing dynamics, emerging trends, and audience feedback.

By following these steps and crafting a comprehensive social media plan, you will be well-positioned to achieve your objectives, connect with your audience authentically, and drive meaningful results for your brand. Embrace the journey, stay flexible, and remember that social media success is a continuous process of refinement and growth.

* * *

Key Takeaways:

- Define specific and measurable goals that align with your brand's vision.
- Develop detailed audience personas to tailor content and engagement strategies effectively.
- Continuously monitor performance metrics and adjust your strategy based on insights to ensure ongoing success.

Action Steps:

- Set SMART goals (Specific, Measurable, Achievable, Relevant, Time-bound) for your social media strategy.
- Create diverse, engaging content that resonates with your audience's interests and preferences.

- Foster genuine interactions with your audience by actively participating in conversations and addressing their needs and concerns.

14

Resources and Tools

Recommended Tools for Content Creation, Scheduling, Analytics, etc.

Content Creation Tools: Effective content creation is at the core of a compelling social media strategy. Consider using tools like Canva or Adobe Spark to elevate your visual content, which provides user-friendly interfaces and many templates for designing engaging graphics, infographics, and social media posts. Unleash your creativity with tools like Piktochart to design visually appealing and informative infographics. Additionally, for captivating multimedia content, try tools like Promo or InVideo to create professional videos without extensive editing skills.

Scheduling Tools: Efficient scheduling is essential for maintaining a consistent social media presence. Platforms like Hootsuite and Buffer allow you to schedule posts across multiple social media channels, streamlining your content distribution strategy. Suppose you're looking for a platform that supports visual planning and collaboration. In that case, tools like Later or Planoly provide a visual calendar for scheduling and previewing posts, ensuring a cohesive and visually appealing feed.

Analytics and Measurement Tools: Accurate analytics tools are indispensable for understanding the impact of your social media efforts. Platforms like Google Analytics offer in-depth insights into website traffic generated from social media, helping you track conversions and user behavior. For a comprehensive view of your social media performance, tools like Sprout Social or Socialbee provide detailed analytics, including engagement metrics, follower growth, and audience demographics. Instagram Insights and Facebook Analytics are powerful native tools that offer detailed statistics on your performance within their respective platforms.

Hashtag Research Tools: Hashtags are crucial in increasing your content's discoverability. Tools like Hashtagify or RiteTag provide insights into trending and relevant hashtags, helping you choose the right ones for your posts. They offer data on hashtag popularity, usage patterns, and related hashtags, allowing you to optimize your content for maximum reach and engagement.

Keyword Research Tools: Incorporating SEO principles into your social media content is crucial for a robust content strategy. Utilize keyword research tools like SEMrush or Ahrefs to identify relevant keywords and phrases. By incorporating these keywords into your social media posts, you enhance your content's discoverability on social platforms and in search engine results.

Influencer Marketing Platforms: If your strategy involves influencer collaboration, platforms like Traackr or AspireIQ help you identify and connect with influencers relevant to your industry. These tools provide insights into influencers' reach, engagement rates, and audience demographics, aiding in strategic partnership decisions.

Integrating these tools into your social media toolkit empowers you to streamline your workflow, enhance the quality of your content, and gain valuable insights for optimizing your strategy. Experiment with different tools to find the best combination with your goals and workflow preferences.

* * *

Key Takeaways:

- Tools can enhance efficiency and effectiveness in social media marketing.
- Continued learning and staying updated are crucial in this rapidly changing field.

Action Steps:

- Research and experiment with tools that align with your needs.
- Explore the recommended resources to deepen your knowledge and skills.

About the Author: Ebony Azuri

From tackling personal decisions to reaching important milestones, Ebony Azuri's passion is guiding individuals and businesses toward success. Fueled by a commitment to excellence, Ebony goes the extra mile to ensure her work satisfies and empowers her clients.

With over a decade of experience as a marketing professional, Ebony has honed her skills in various industries, including nonprofits, healthcare, and finance. Her journey in the marketing realm has equipped her with a profound understanding of the ever-evolving landscape and the strategies that resonate across diverse sectors.

As a seasoned Marketing Consultant, Ebony believes in the power of a positive mindset and the impact of purposeful partnerships. Her approach is not just about delivering services; it's about crafting collaborative strategies that lead to significant outcomes. Whether building brand awareness, driving engagement, or navigating the complexities of digital marketing, Ebony's expertise lies in translating ideas into actionable and impactful campaigns.

Ebony's dedication to her craft is evident in her professional endeavors and extends to her latest work, "Social Media Mastery: Crafting Your Blueprint for Success." This book is a culmination of her extensive knowledge and practical insights gained over the years, offering readers a comprehensive guide to navigate and excel in the world of social media.

Join Ebony on this journey of strategic exploration, where she shares the keys to mastering social media, fostering authentic connections, and crafting compelling narratives that resonate in the digital landscape. Her commitment to your success is not just a professional ethos; it reflects her passion for empowering others on their unique paths.

www.ingramcontent.com/pod-product-compliance
Lightning Source LLC
Chambersburg PA
CBHW042102150726
48005CB00033B/1597